This book belongs to

Email / Telephone

I recommend using sticky note markers to bookmark the current page/week.

What is ARFID?

Avoidant restrictive food intake disorder (ARFID) is an eating disorder similar to anorexia. Both conditions involve intense restrictions on the amount of food and types of foods you eat, unlike anorexia, people with ARFID aren't worried about their body image, shape, or size.

Many children will have phases of picky eating. But ARFID which used to be called selective eating disorder is different. Someone with ARFID will simply starve rather than trying unfamiliar foods, In children, this can lead to delayed weight gain and growth.

Doctors don't know what causes ARFID. Some experts believe that people who get it might have extreme sensitivity to taste or texture. They might have had a bad experience with food like choking or vomiting that makes them fearful or anxious about food.

People most likely to have ARFID include:

Children who never outgrow picky eating
People on the autism spectrum
Those with ADHD
Anxiety Disorders

To confirm if you have ARFID, you must see your doctor who will ask questions about your eating habits.

I designed this journal to help log this information which should help with a diagnosis and also to help you along on your journey.

Me

When my ARFID began:

My safe foods

-
-
-

-
-
-

-
-
-

-
-
-

Triggers/Cause?

Any other diagnoses/Disorders/Phobias

Concerns while eating?

Nutritional Supplements I take

Usual daily tasks

Tasks I struggle with

Example of the daily food log

Today's Date: __Monday 27th September__

Breakfast

cereal

Lunch

Ham Sandwich

Dinner

chicken nuggets + Fries

New Foods(s)I tried today....

cheese Omelette

Textures

creamy, Smooth, Gooey, soft

Smell

Quite strong egg + cheese

Color

Yellow + Orange

Hot or Cold

Hot

Monday

B _____
L _____
D _____

Tuesday

B _____
L _____
D _____

Wednesday

B _____
L _____
D _____

Thursday

B _____
L _____
D _____

Friday

B _____
L _____
D _____

Saturday

B _____
L _____
D _____

Sunday

B _____
L _____
D _____

Date _____

Grocery List

Fruits & Veggies	Dairy
Meat	Frozen
Ingredients	Snacks

Snacks

_____
_____
_____
_____
_____

My Goals!

Week:

This weeks Goals

To Do List

Notes

<u>Daily Food Log</u>

Today's Date: _ _ _ _ _ _ _ _ _ _ _ _ _ _ _ _ _ _

Breakfast

New Foods(s)I tried today....

Lunch

Textures

Dinner

Smell

Color

Hot or Cold

<u>Daily Food Log</u>

Today's Date: _

Breakfast

New Foods(s)I tried today....

Lunch

Textures

Smell

Dinner

Color

Hot or Cold

Daily Food Log

Today's Date: _ _ _ _ _ _ _ _ _ _ _ _ _ _ _ _ _ _ _

Breakfast

Lunch

Dinner

New Foods(s)I tried today....

Textures

Smell

Color

Hot or Cold

<u>Daily Food Log</u>

Today's Date: _ _ _ _ _ _ _ _ _ _ _ _ _ _ _ _ _ _

Breakfast

New Foods(s)I tried today....

Lunch

Textures

Smell

Dinner

Color

Hot or Cold

Daily Food Log

Today's Date: _

Breakfast

New Foods(s)I tried today....

Lunch

Textures

Dinner

Smell

Color

Hot or Cold

<u>Daily Food Log</u>

Today's Date: _ _ _ _ _ _ _ _ _ _ _ _ _ _ _ _ _ _ _

Breakfast

New Foods(s)I tried today....

Lunch

Textures

Smell

Dinner

Color

Hot or Cold

<u>Daily Food Log</u>

Today's Date: _ _ _ _ _ _ _ _ _ _ _ _ _ _ _ _ _

Breakfast

New Foods(s)I tried today....

Lunch

Textures

Smell

Dinner

Color

Hot or Cold

My Weekly Emotions Log

Date:

Choose two words from the list to describe how you felt this week. Feel free to use other words.

What can cheer you up or help you stay happy and focused?

angry
annoyed
anxious
ashamed
awkward
brave
calm
cheerful
chill
confused
discouraged
disgusted
distracted
embarrassed
excited
friendly
guilty
happy
hopeful
jealous
lonely
loved
nervous
offended
scared
thoughtful
tired
uncomfortable
unsure
worried

Anxiety Log

Date _____ Source of Anxiety _____

Time _____ Physical Sensations _____

Place _____

Negative Beliefs

About Yourself	About Situation

What facts do you know are true?

About Yourself	About Situation

Color where you feel
sensations of anxiety

Is there a more balanced way to think about this situation

What has helped before?

What is helping now?

Coping Mechanisms

Breathe
Remind yourself that anxiety is just a feeling
Describe your surroundings in detail
Go outdoors
Sip a warm or iced drink slowly
Ground yourself

Monday
B _____
L _____
D _____

Tuesday
B _____
L _____
D _____

Wednesday
B _____
L _____
D _____

Thursday
B _____
L _____
D _____

Friday
B _____
L _____
D _____

Saturday
B _____
L _____
D _____

Sunday
B _____
L _____
D _____

Date _____

Grocery List

Fruits & Veggies	Dairy
Meat	Frozen
Ingredients	Snacks

Snacks

_____
_____
_____
_____
_____

My Goals!

Week:

This weeks Goals

To Do List

Notes

Daily Food Log

Today's Date: _

Breakfast

New Foods(s)I tried today....

Lunch

Textures

Smell

Dinner

Color

Hot or Cold

Daily Food Log

Today's Date: _ _ _ _ _ _ _ _ _ _ _ _ _ _ _ _ _ _ _

Breakfast

New Foods(s)I tried today....

Lunch

Textures

Dinner

Smell

Color

Hot or Cold

Daily Food Log

Today's Date: _ _ _ _ _ _ _ _ _ _ _ _ _ _ _ _ _ _ _

Breakfast

New Foods(s)I tried today....

Lunch

Textures

Smell

Dinner

Color

Hot or Cold

Daily Food Log

Today's Date: _ _ _ _ _ _ _ _ _ _ _ _ _ _ _ _ _ _

Breakfast

New Foods(s)I tried today....

Lunch

Textures

Smell

Dinner

Color

Hot or Cold

<u>Daily Food Log</u>

Today's Date: _ _ _ _ _ _ _ _ _ _ _ _ _ _ _ _ _ _ _

Breakfast

New Foods(s)I tried today....

Lunch

Textures

Smell

Dinner

Color

Hot or Cold

Daily Food Log

Today's Date: _ _ _ _ _ _ _ _ _ _ _ _ _ _ _ _ _ _ _

Breakfast

New Foods(s)I tried today....

Lunch

Textures

Smell

Dinner

Color

Hot or Cold

<u>Daily Food Log</u>

Today's Date: _ _ _ _ _ _ _ _ _ _ _ _ _ _ _ _ _ _ _

Breakfast

New Foods(s)I tried today....

Lunch

Textures

Smell

Dinner

Color

Hot or Cold

My Weekly Emotions Log

Date:	

Choose two words from the list to describe how you felt this week. Feel free to use other words.

What can cheer you up or help you stay happy and focused?

angry
annoyed
anxious
ashamed
awkward
brave
calm
cheerful
chill
confused
discouraged
disgusted
distracted
embarrassed
excited
friendly
guilty
happy
hopeful
jealous
lonely
loved
nervous
offended
scared
thoughtful
tired
uncomfortable
unsure
worried

Anxiety Log

Date _____   Source of Anxiety _____

Time _____   Physical Sensations _____

Place _____

Negative Beliefs

About Yourself	About Situation

What facts do you know are true?

About Yourself	About Situation

Color where you feel
sensations of anxiety

Is there a more balanced way to think about this situation

What has helped before?   ## What is helping now?

Coping Mechanisms

Breathe
Remind yourself that anxiety is just a feeling
Describe your surroundings in detail
Go outdoors
Sip a warm or iced drink slowly
Ground yourself

Monday

B _____
L _____
D _____

Tuesday

B _____
L _____
D _____

Wednesday

B _____
L _____
D _____

Thursday

B _____
L _____
D _____

Friday

B _____
L _____
D _____

Saturday

B _____
L _____
D _____

Sunday

B _____
L _____
D _____

Date _____

Grocery List

Fruits & Veggies	Dairy
Meat	Frozen
Ingredients	Snacks

Snacks

_____
_____
_____
_____
_____

My Goals!

Week:

This weeks Goals

To Do List

Notes

Daily Food Log

Today's Date: _ _ _ _ _ _ _ _ _ _ _ _ _ _ _ _ _ _ _

Breakfast

New Foods(s)I tried today....

Lunch

Textures

Smell

Dinner

Color

Hot or Cold

Daily Food Log

Today's Date: _ _ _ _ _ _ _ _ _ _ _ _ _ _ _ _ _ _ _

Breakfast

New Foods(s)I tried today....

Lunch

Textures

Smell

Dinner

Color

Hot or Cold

<u>Daily Food Log</u>

Today's Date:

Breakfast

New Foods(s) I tried today....

Lunch

Textures

Dinner

Smell

Color

Hot or Cold

Daily Food Log

Today's Date: _ _ _ _ _ _ _ _ _ _ _ _ _ _ _ _ _ _ _

Breakfast

New Foods(s)I tried today....

Lunch

Textures

Smell

Dinner

Color

Hot or Cold

Daily Food Log

Today's Date: _ _ _ _ _ _ _ _ _ _ _ _ _ _ _ _ _ _ _

Breakfast

New Foods(s)I tried today....

Lunch

Textures

Smell

Dinner

Color

Hot or Cold

<u>Daily Food Log</u>

Today's Date: _ _ _ _ _ _ _ _ _ _ _ _ _ _ _ _ _ _

Breakfast

New Foods(s)I tried today....

Lunch

Textures

Smell

Dinner

Color

Hot or Cold

Daily Food Log

Today's Date: _ _ _ _ _ _ _ _ _ _ _ _ _ _ _ _ _ _ _

Breakfast

New Foods(s)I tried today....

Lunch

Textures

Smell

Dinner

Color

Hot or Cold

<u>My Weekly Emotions Log</u>

Date:

Choose two words from the list to describe how you felt this week. Feel free to use other words.

What can cheer you up or help you stay happy and focused?

angry
annoyed
anxious
ashamed
awkward
brave
calm
cheerful
chill
confused
discouraged
disgusted
distracted
embarrassed
excited
friendly
guilty
happy
hopeful
jealous
lonely
loved
nervous
offended
scared
thoughtful
tired
uncomfortable
unsure
worried

Anxiety Log

Date _____   Source of Anxiety _____

Time _____   Physical Sensations _____

Place _____

Negative Beliefs

About Yourself	About Situation

What facts do you know are true?

About Yourself	About Situation

Color where you feel
sensations of anxiety

Is there a more balanced way to think about this situation

What has helped before?   ## What is helping now?

Coping Mechanisms

Breathe
Remind yourself that anxiety is just a feeling
Describe your surroundings in detail
Go outdoors
Sip a warm or iced drink slowly
Ground yourself

Monday

B _____
L _____
D _____

Tuesday

B _____
L _____
D _____

Wednesday

B _____
L _____
D _____

Thursday

B _____
L _____
D _____

Friday

B _____
L _____
D _____

Saturday

B _____
L _____
D _____

Sunday

B _____
L _____
D _____

Date _____

Grocery List

Fruits & Veggies	Dairy
Meat	Frozen
Ingredients	Snacks

Snacks

_____
_____
_____
_____

My Goals!

Week:

This weeks Goals

To Do List

Notes

<u>Daily Food Log</u>

Today's Date: _ _ _ _ _ _ _ _ _ _ _ _ _ _ _ _ _ _ _

Breakfast

New Foods(s)I tried today....

Lunch

Textures

Smell

Dinner

Color

Hot or Cold

Daily Food Log

Today's Date: _

Breakfast

Lunch

Dinner

New Foods(s)I tried today....

Textures

Smell

Color

Hot or Cold

Daily Food Log

Today's Date: _ _ _ _ _ _ _ _ _ _ _ _ _ _ _ _ _ _ _

Breakfast

New Foods(s)I tried today....

Lunch

Textures

Smell

Dinner

Color

Hot or Cold

<u>Daily Food Log</u>

Today's Date: _ _ _ _ _ _ _ _ _ _ _ _ _ _ _ _ _ _ _

Breakfast

New Foods(s)I tried today....

Lunch

Textures

Smell

Dinner

Color

Hot or Cold

<u>Daily Food Log</u>

Today's Date: _ _ _ _ _ _ _ _ _ _ _ _ _ _ _ _ _ _ _

Breakfast

Lunch

Dinner

New Foods(s)I tried today....

Textures

Smell

Color

Hot or Cold

<u>Daily Food Log</u>

Today's Date: _ _ _ _ _ _ _ _ _ _ _ _ _ _ _ _ _ _ _

Breakfast

New Foods(s)I tried today....

Lunch

Textures

Smell

Dinner

Color

Hot or Cold

<u>Daily Food Log</u>

Today's Date: _____

Breakfast

New Foods(s)I tried today....

Lunch

Textures

Smell

Dinner

Color

Hot or Cold

My Weekly Emotions Log

Date:

Choose two words from the list to describe how you felt this week. Feel free to use other words.

What can cheer you up or help you stay happy and focused?

angry
annoyed
anxious
ashamed
awkward
brave
calm
cheerful
chill
confused
discouraged
disgusted
distracted
embarrassed
excited
friendly
guilty
happy
hopeful
jealous
lonely
loved
nervous
offended
scared
thoughtful
tired
uncomfortable
unsure
worried

Anxiety Log

Date _____   Source of Anxiety _____

Time _____   Physical Sensations _____

Place _____

Negative Beliefs

About Yourself	About Situation

What facts do you know are true?

About Yourself	About Situation

Color where you feel
sensations of anxiety

Is there a more balanced way to think about this situation

What has helped before?   What is helping now?

—— Coping Mechanisms ——

Breathe
Remind yourself that anxiety is just a feeling
Describe your surroundings in detail
Go outdoors
Sip a warm or iced drink slowly
Ground yourself

Monday
B _____
L _____
D _____

Tuesday
B _____
L _____
D _____

Wednesday
B _____
L _____
D _____

Thursday
B _____
L _____
D _____

Friday
B _____
L _____
D _____

Saturday
B _____
L _____
D _____

Sunday
B _____
L _____
D _____

Date _____

Grocery List

Fruits & Veggies	Dairy
Meat	Frozen
Ingredients	Snacks

Snacks
_____
_____
_____
_____
_____

My Goals!

Week:

This weeks Goals

To Do List

Notes

Daily Food Log

Today's Date: _ _ _ _ _ _ _ _ _ _ _ _ _ _ _ _ _ _ _

Breakfast

New Foods(s) I tried today....

Lunch

Textures

Smell

Dinner

Color

Hot or Cold

<u>Daily Food Log</u>

Today's Date: _ _ _ _ _ _ _ _ _ _ _ _ _ _ _ _ _ _

Breakfast

New Foods(s)I tried today....

Lunch

Textures

Smell

Dinner

Color

Hot or Cold

<u>Daily Food Log</u>

Today's Date: _ _ _ _ _ _ _ _ _ _ _ _ _ _ _ _ _ _

Breakfast

New Foods(s)I tried today....

Lunch

Textures

Smell

Dinner

Color

Hot or Cold

Daily Food Log

Today's Date: _ _ _ _ _ _ _ _ _ _ _ _ _ _ _ _ _ _ _

Breakfast

New Foods(s)I tried today....

Lunch

Textures

Smell

Dinner

Color

Hot or Cold

Daily Food Log

Today's Date: _ _ _ _ _ _ _ _ _ _ _ _ _ _ _ _ _

Breakfast

New Foods(s) I tried today....

Lunch

Textures

Smell

Dinner

Color

Hot or Cold

<u>Daily Food Log</u>

Today's Date: _ _ _ _ _ _ _ _ _ _ _ _ _ _ _ _ _ _ _

Breakfast

New Foods(s)I tried today....

Lunch

Textures

Smell

Dinner

Color

Hot or Cold

Daily Food Log

Today's Date: - - - - - - - - - - - - - - - - - - -

Breakfast

New Foods(s)I tried today....

Lunch

Textures

Smell

Dinner

Color

Hot or Cold

My Weekly Emotions Log

Date:

Choose two words from the list to describe how you felt this week. Feel free to use other words.

What can cheer you up or help you stay happy and focused?

angry
annoyed
anxious
ashamed
awkward
brave
calm
cheerful
chill
confused
discouraged
disgusted
distracted
embarrassed
excited
friendly
guilty
happy
hopeful
jealous
lonely
loved
nervous
offended
scared
thoughtful
tired
uncomfortable
unsure
worried

<u>Anxiety Log</u>

Date _____   Source of Anxiety _____

Time _____   Physical Sensations _____

Place _____

Negative Beliefs

About Yourself	About Situation

What facts do you know are true?

About Yourself	About Situation

Color where you feel
sensations of anxiety

Is there a more balanced way to think about this situation

What has helped before?   What is helping now?

———— Coping Mechanisms ————

Breathe
Remind yourself that anxiety is just a feeling
Describe your surroundings in detail
Go outdoors
Sip a warm or iced drink slowly
Ground yourself

Monday

B _____
L _____
D _____

Tuesday

B _____
L _____
D _____

Wednesday

B _____
L _____
D _____

Thursday

B _____
L _____
D _____

Friday

B _____
L _____
D _____

Saturday

B _____
L _____
D _____

Sunday

B _____
L _____
D _____

Date _____

Grocery List

Fruits & Veggies	Dairy
Meat	Frozen
Ingredients	Snacks

Snacks

My Goals!

Week:

This weeks Goals

To Do List

Notes

Daily Food Log

Today's Date: _

Breakfast

New Foods(s)I tried today....

Lunch

Textures

Smell

Dinner

Color

Hot or Cold

<u>Daily Food Log</u>

Today's Date: _ _ _ _ _ _ _ _ _ _ _ _ _ _ _ _ _ _

Breakfast

New Foods(s)I tried today....

Lunch

Textures

Smell

Dinner

Color

Hot or Cold

<u>Daily Food Log</u>

Today's Date: _ _ _ _ _ _ _ _ _ _ _ _ _ _ _ _ _ _ _

Breakfast

Lunch

Dinner

New Foods(s)I tried today....

Textures

Smell

Color

Hot or Cold

Daily Food Log

Today's Date: _ _ _ _ _ _ _ _ _ _ _ _ _ _ _ _ _

Breakfast

New Foods(s) I tried today....

Lunch

Textures

Smell

Dinner

Color

Hot or Cold

<u>Daily Food Log</u>

Today's Date: _ _ _ _ _ _ _ _ _ _ _ _ _ _ _ _ _ _

Breakfast

New Foods(s)I tried today....

Lunch

Textures

Smell

Dinner

Color

Hot or Cold

Daily Food Log

Today's Date: _ _ _ _ _ _ _ _ _ _ _ _ _ _ _ _ _ _ _

Breakfast

New Foods(s)I tried today....

Lunch

Textures

Smell

Dinner

Color

Hot or Cold

<u>Daily</u> Food Log

Today's Date: _ _ _ _ _ _ _ _ _ _ _ _ _ _ _ _ _ _ _

Breakfast

New Foods(s) I tried today....

Lunch

Textures

Smell

Dinner

Color

Hot or Cold

My Weekly Emotions Log

Date:	

Choose two words from the list to describe how you felt this week. Feel free to use other words.

What can cheer you up or help you stay happy and focused?

angry
annoyed
anxious
ashamed
awkward
brave
calm
cheerful
chill
confused
discouraged
disgusted
distracted
embarrassed
excited
friendly
guilty
happy
hopeful
jealous
lonely
loved
nervous
offended
scared
thoughtful
tired
uncomfortable
unsure
worried

Anxiety Log

Date _____   Source of Anxiety _____

Time _____   Physical Sensations _____

Place _____

Negative Beliefs

About Yourself	About Situation

What facts do you know are true?

About Yourself	About Situation

Color where you feel
sensations of anxiety

Is there a more balanced way to think about this situation

What has helped before?

What is helping now?

——— Coping Mechanisms ———

Breathe
Remind yourself that anxiety is just a feeling
Describe your surroundings in detail
Go outdoors
Sip a warm or iced drink slowly
Ground yourself

Monday

B _____
L _____
D _____

Tuesday

B _____
L _____
D _____

Wednesday

B _____
L _____
D _____

Thursday

B _____
L _____
D _____

Friday

B _____
L _____
D _____

Saturday

B _____
L _____
D _____

Sunday

B _____
L _____
D _____

Date _____

Grocery List

Fruits & Veggies	Dairy
Meat	Frozen
Ingredients	Snacks

Snacks

_____
_____
_____
_____
_____

My Goals!

Week:

This weeks Goals

To Do List

Notes

<u>Daily Food Log</u>

Today's Date: _ _ _ _ _ _ _ _ _ _ _ _ _ _ _ _ _ _

Breakfast

New Foods(s)I tried today....

Lunch

Textures

Smell

Dinner

Color

Hot or Cold

<u>Daily Food Log</u>

Today's Date: _ _ _ _ _ _ _ _ _ _ _ _ _ _ _ _ _ _ _

Breakfast

New Foods(s)I tried today....

Lunch

Textures

Smell

Dinner

Color

Hot or Cold

<u>Daily Food Log</u>

Today's Date: _ _ _ _ _ _ _ _ _ _ _ _ _ _ _ _ _ _ _

Breakfast

New Foods(s)I tried today....

Lunch

Textures

Dinner

Smell

Color

Hot or Cold

<u>Daily Food Log</u>

Today's Date: _ _ _ _ _ _ _ _ _ _ _ _ _ _ _ _ _

Breakfast

New Foods(s)I tried today....

Lunch

Textures

Smell

Dinner

Color

Hot or Cold

<u>Daily Food Log</u>

Today's Date: _

Breakfast

New Foods(s)I tried today....

Lunch

Textures

Smell

Dinner

Color

Hot or Cold

<u>Daily Food Log</u>

Today's Date: _ _ _ _ _ _ _ _ _ _ _ _ _ _ _ _ _ _ _

Breakfast

New Foods(s)I tried today....

Lunch

Textures

Smell

Dinner

Color

Hot or Cold

<u>Daily Food Log</u>

Today's Date: _____

Breakfast

New Foods(s)I tried today....

Lunch

Textures

Dinner

Smell

Color

Hot or Cold

My Weekly Emotions Log

Date:	

Choose two words from the list to describe how you felt this week. Feel free to use other words.

What can cheer you up or help you stay happy and focused?

angry
annoyed
anxious
ashamed
awkward
brave
calm
cheerful
chill
confused
discouraged
disgusted
distracted
embarrassed
excited
friendly
guilty
happy
hopeful
jealous
lonely
loved
nervous
offended
scared
thoughtful
tired
uncomfortable
unsure
worried

<u>Anxiety Log</u>

Date _____   Source of Anxiety _____

Time _____   Physical Sensations _____

Place _____

Negative Beliefs

About Yourself	About Situation

What facts do you know are true?

About Yourself	About Situation

Color where you feel
sensations of anxiety

Is there a more balanced way to think about this situation

What has helped before?   What is helping now?

──── Coping Mechanisms ────

Breathe
Remind yourself that anxiety is just a feeling
Describe your surroundings in detail
Go outdoors
Sip a warm or iced drink slowly
Ground yourself

Monday

B _____
L _____
D _____

Tuesday

B _____
L _____
D _____

Wednesday

B _____
L _____
D _____

Thursday

B _____
L _____
D _____

Friday

B _____
L _____
D _____

Saturday

B _____
L _____
D _____

Sunday

B _____
L _____
D _____

Date _____

Grocery List

Fruits & Veggies	Dairy
Meat	Frozen
Ingredients	Snacks

Snacks

_____
_____
_____
_____

My Goals!

Week:

This weeks Goals

To Do List

Notes

<u>Daily Food Log</u>

Today's Date: _ _ _ _ _ _ _ _ _ _ _ _ _ _ _ _ _ _

Breakfast

New Foods(s)I tried today....

Lunch

Textures

Smell

Dinner

Color

Hot or Cold

Daily Food Log

Today's Date: _____

Breakfast

New Foods(s)I tried today....

Lunch

Textures

Smell

Dinner

Color

Hot or Cold

Daily Food Log

Today's Date: _ _ _ _ _ _ _ _ _ _ _ _ _ _ _ _ _ _ _

Breakfast

New Foods(s)I tried today....

Lunch

Textures

Smell

Dinner

Color

Hot or Cold

Daily Food Log

Today's Date: _ _ _ _ _ _ _ _ _ _ _ _ _ _ _ _ _ _

Breakfast

New Foods(s)I tried today....

Lunch

Textures

Smell

Dinner

Color

Hot or Cold

Daily Food Log

Today's Date: _ _ _ _ _ _ _ _ _ _ _ _ _ _ _ _ _ _

Breakfast

New Foods(s)I tried today....

Lunch

Textures

Smell

Dinner

Color

Hot or Cold

Daily Food Log

Today's Date: - - - - - - - - - - - - - - - - - - -

Breakfast

New Foods(s)I tried today....

Lunch

Textures

Smell

Dinner

Color

Hot or Cold

<u>Daily Food Log</u>

Today's Date: _

Breakfast

New Foods(s)I tried today....

Lunch

Textures

Smell

Dinner

Color

Hot or Cold

My Weekly Emotions Log

Date:	

Choose two words from the list to describe
how you felt this week. Feel free to use other
words.

**What can cheer you up or help you stay
happy and focused?**

angry
annoyed
anxious
ashamed
awkward
brave
calm
cheerful
chill
confused
discouraged
disgusted
distracted
embarrassed
excited
friendly
guilty
happy
hopeful
jealous
lonely
loved
nervous
offended
scared
thoughtful
tired
uncomfortable
unsure
worried

<u>Anxiety Log</u>

Date _____   Source of Anxiety _____

Time _____   Physical Sensations _____

Place _____

Negative Beliefs

About Yourself	About Situation

What facts do you know are true?

About Yourself	About Situation

Color where you feel
sensations of anxiety

Is there a more balanced way to think about this situation

What has helped before?   What is helping now?

────── Coping Mechanisms ──────
Breathe
Remind yourself that anxiety is just a feeling
Describe your surroundings in detail
Go outdoors
Sip a warm or iced drink slowly
Ground yourself

Monday

B
L
D

Tuesday

B
L
D

Wednesday

B
L
D

Thursday

B
L
D

Friday

B
L
D

Saturday

B
L
D

Sunday

B
L
D

Date

Grocery List

Fruits & Veggies	Dairy
Meat	Frozen
Ingredients	Snacks

Snacks

My Goals!

Week:

This weeks Goals

To Do List

Notes

Daily Food Log

Today's Date: _ _ _ _ _ _ _ _ _ _ _ _ _ _ _ _ _ _ _

Breakfast

New Foods(s) I tried today....

Lunch

Textures

Smell

Dinner

Color

Hot or Cold

Daily Food Log

Today's Date: _ _ _ _ _ _ _ _ _ _ _ _ _ _ _ _ _ _

Breakfast

New Foods(s)I tried today....

Lunch

Textures

Smell

Dinner

Color

Hot or Cold

Daily Food Log

Today's Date: -

Breakfast

New Foods(s)I tried today....

Lunch

Textures

Smell

Dinner

Color

Hot or Cold

Daily Food Log

Today's Date: _

Breakfast

New Foods(s)I tried today....

Lunch

Textures

Smell

Dinner

Color

Hot or Cold

Daily Food Log

Today's Date: _

Breakfast

New Foods(s)I tried today....

Lunch

Textures

Smell

Dinner

Color

Hot or Cold

Daily Food Log

Today's Date: _

Breakfast

New Foods(s)I tried today....

Lunch

Textures

Smell

Dinner

Color

Hot or Cold

Daily Food Log

Today's Date: _____

Breakfast

New Foods(s) I tried today....

Lunch

Textures

Dinner

Smell

Color

Hot or Cold

My Weekly Emotions Log

Date:

Choose two words from the list to describe how you felt this week. Feel free to use other words.

What can cheer you up or help you stay happy and focused?

angry
annoyed
anxious
ashamed
awkward
brave
calm
cheerful
chill
confused
discouraged
disgusted
distracted
embarrassed
excited
friendly
guilty
happy
hopeful
jealous
lonely
loved
nervous
offended
scared
thoughtful
tired
uncomfortable
unsure
worried

Anxiety Log

Date _____   Source of Anxiety _____

Time _____   Physical Sensations _____

Place _____

Negative Beliefs

About Yourself	About Situation

What facts do you know are true?

About Yourself	About Situation

Color where you feel
sensations of anxiety

Is there a more balanced way to think about this situation

What has helped before?   What is helping now?

——— Coping Mechanisms ———

Breathe
Remind yourself that anxiety is just a feeling
Describe your surroundings in detail
Go outdoors
Sip a warm or iced drink slowly
Ground yourself

Monday

B _____
L _____
D _____

Tuesday

B _____
L _____
D _____

Wednesday

B _____
L _____
D _____

Thursday

B _____
L _____
D _____

Friday

B _____
L _____
D _____

Saturday

B _____
L _____
D _____

Sunday

B _____
L _____
D _____

Date _____

Grocery List

Fruits & Veggies	Dairy
Meat	Frozen
Ingredients	Snacks

Snacks

_____
_____
_____
_____
_____

My Goals!

Week:

This weeks Goals

To Do List

Notes

<u>Daily Food Log</u>

Today's Date: _ _ _ _ _ _ _ _ _ _ _ _ _ _ _ _

Breakfast

Lunch

Dinner

New Foods(s)I tried today....

Textures

Smell

Color

Hot or Cold

<u>Daily Food Log</u>

Today's Date: _

Breakfast

New Foods(s)I tried today....

Lunch

Textures

Dinner

Smell

Color

Hot or Cold

Daily Food Log

Today's Date: _ _ _ _ _ _ _ _ _ _ _ _ _ _ _ _ _ _

Breakfast

New Foods(s)I tried today....

Lunch

Textures

Smell

Dinner

Color

Hot or Cold

Daily Food Log

Today's Date: _ _ _ _ _ _ _ _ _ _ _ _ _ _ _ _ _ _ _

Breakfast

New Foods(s)I tried today....

Lunch

Textures

Smell

Dinner

Color

Hot or Cold

<u>Daily Food Log</u>

Today's Date: _

Breakfast

New Foods(s)I tried today....

Lunch

Textures

Dinner

Smell

Color

Hot or Cold

<u>Daily Food Log</u>

Today's Date: _ _ _ _ _ _ _ _ _ _ _ _ _ _ _ _ _ _ _

Breakfast

New Foods(s)I tried today....

Lunch

Textures

Smell

Dinner

Color

Hot or Cold

<u>Daily Food Log</u>

Today's Date: - - - - - - - - - - - - - - - - - - -

Breakfast

New Foods(s)I tried today....

Lunch

Textures

Smell

Dinner

Color

Hot or Cold

<u>My Weekly Emotions Log</u>

Date:	

Choose two words from the list to describe how you felt this week. Feel free to use other words.

What can cheer you up or help you stay happy and focused?

angry
annoyed
anxious
ashamed
awkward
brave
calm
cheerful
chill
confused
discouraged
disgusted
distracted
embarrassed
excited
friendly
guilty
happy
hopeful
jealous
lonely
loved
nervous
offended
scared
thoughtful
tired
uncomfortable
unsure
worried

Anxiety Log

Date _____   Source of Anxiety _____

Time _____   Physical Sensations _____

Place _____

Negative Beliefs

About Yourself	About Situation

What facts do you know are true?

About Yourself	About Situation

Color where you feel
sensations of anxiety

Is there a more balanced way to think about this situation

What has helped before?

What is helping now?

Coping Mechanisms

Breathe
Remind yourself that anxiety is just a feeling
Describe your surroundings in detail
Go outdoors
Sip a warm or iced drink slowly
Ground yourself

Monday

B _____
L _____
D _____

Tuesday

B _____
L _____
D _____

Wednesday

B _____
L _____
D _____

Thursday

B _____
L _____
D _____

Friday

B _____
L _____
D _____

Saturday

B _____
L _____
D _____

Sunday

B _____
L _____
D _____

Date _____

Grocery List

Fruits & Veggies	Dairy
Meat	Frozen
Ingredients	Snacks

Snacks

_____
_____
_____
_____
_____

My Goals!

Week:

This weeks Goals

To Do List

Notes

Daily Food Log

Today's Date: _

Breakfast

New Foods(s)I tried today....

Lunch

Textures

Smell

Dinner

Color

Hot or Cold

Daily Food Log

Today's Date: _ _ _ _ _ _ _ _ _ _ _ _ _ _ _ _ _ _ _

Breakfast

New Foods(s)I tried today....

Lunch

Textures

Smell

Dinner

Color

Hot or Cold

Daily Food Log

Today's Date: - - - - - - - - - - - - - - - - - - -

Breakfast

New Foods(s)I tried today....

Lunch

Textures

Smell

Dinner

Color

Hot or Cold

<u>Daily Food Log</u>

Today's Date: _ _ _ _ _ _ _ _ _ _ _ _ _ _ _ _ _ _ _

Breakfast

New Foods(s)I tried today....

Lunch

Textures

Smell

Dinner

Color

Hot or Cold

<u>Daily Food Log</u>

Today's Date: _ _ _ _ _ _ _ _ _ _ _ _ _ _ _ _ _ _ _

Breakfast

New Foods(s)I tried today....

Lunch

Textures

Smell

Dinner

Color

Hot or Cold

Daily Food Log

Today's Date: _ _ _ _ _ _ _ _ _ _ _ _ _ _ _ _ _ _ _

Breakfast

New Foods(s)I tried today....

Lunch

Textures

Smell

Dinner

Color

Hot or Cold

<u>Daily Food Log</u>

Today's Date: _ _ _ _ _ _ _ _ _ _ _ _ _ _ _ _ _ _ _

Breakfast

New Foods(s)I tried today....

Lunch

Textures

Smell

Dinner

Color

Hot or Cold

My Weekly Emotions Log

Date:

Choose two words from the list to describe how you felt this week. Feel free to use other words.

What can cheer you up or help you stay happy and focused?

angry
annoyed
anxious
ashamed
awkward
brave
calm
cheerful
chill
confused
discouraged
disgusted
distracted
embarrassed
excited
friendly
guilty
happy
hopeful
jealous
lonely
loved
nervous
offended
scared
thoughtful
tired
uncomfortable
unsure
worried

Anxiety Log

Date _____   Source of Anxiety _____

Time _____   Physical Sensations _____

Place _____

Negative Beliefs

About Yourself	About Situation

What facts do you know are true?

About Yourself	About Situation

Color where you feel
sensations of anxiety

Is there a more balanced way to think about this situation

What has helped before?   What is helping now?

────── Coping Mechanisms ──────

Breathe
Remind yourself that anxiety is just a feeling
Describe your surroundings in detail
Go outdoors
Sip a warm or iced drink slowly
Ground yourself

Monday

B _____
L _____
D _____

Tuesday

B _____
L _____
D _____

Wednesday

B _____
L _____
D _____

Thursday

B _____
L _____
D _____

Friday

B _____
L _____
D _____

Saturday

B _____
L _____
D _____

Sunday

B _____
L _____
D _____

Date _____

Grocery List

Fruits & Veggies	Dairy
Meat	Frozen
Ingredients	Snacks

Snacks

_____
_____
_____
_____
_____

My Goals!

Week:

This weeks Goals

To Do List

Notes

Daily Food Log

Today's Date: _ _ _ _ _ _ _ _ _ _ _ _ _ _ _ _ _ _ _

Breakfast

New Foods(s)I tried today....

Lunch

Textures

Smell

Dinner

Color

Hot or Cold

<u>Daily Food Log</u>

Today's Date: _

Breakfast

New Foods(s)I tried today....

Lunch

Textures

Smell

Dinner

Color

Hot or Cold

Daily Food Log

Today's Date: _ _ _ _ _ _ _ _ _ _ _ _ _ _ _ _ _ _ _

Breakfast

New Foods(s)I tried today....

Lunch

Textures

Smell

Dinner

Color

Hot or Cold

Daily Food Log

Today's Date: _____

Breakfast

New Foods(s) I tried today....

Lunch

Textures

Dinner

Smell

Color

Hot or Cold

<u>Daily Food Log</u>

Today's Date: _ _ _ _ _ _ _ _ _ _ _ _ _ _ _ _ _

Breakfast

New Foods(s)I tried today....

Lunch

Textures

Smell

Dinner

Color

Hot or Cold

<u>Daily Food Log</u>

Today's Date: _

Breakfast

New Foods(s)I tried today....

Lunch

Textures

Smell

Dinner

Color

Hot or Cold

<u>Daily Food Log</u>

Today's Date: _ _ _ _ _ _ _ _ _ _ _ _ _ _ _ _ _ _ _

Breakfast

New Foods(s)I tried today....

Lunch

Textures

Smell

Dinner

Color

Hot or Cold

<u>My Weekly Emotions Log</u>

Date:	

Choose two words from the list to describe how you felt this week. Feel free to use other words.

angry
annoyed
anxious
ashamed
awkward
brave
calm
cheerful
chill
confused
discouraged
disgusted
distracted
embarrassed
excited
friendly
guilty
happy
hopeful
jealous
lonely
loved
nervous
offended
scared
thoughtful
tired
uncomfortable
unsure
worried

What can cheer you up or help you stay happy and focused?

Anxiety Log

Date _____   Source of Anxiety _____

Time _____   Physical Sensations _____

Place _____

Negative Beliefs

About Yourself	About Situation

What facts do you know are true?

About Yourself	About Situation

Color where you feel
sensations of anxiety

Is there a more balanced way to think about this situation

What has helped before?   What is helping now?

———— Coping Mechanisms ————

Breathe
Remind yourself that anxiety is just a feeling
Describe your surroundings in detail
Go outdoors
Sip a warm or iced drink slowly
Ground yourself

Monday

B _____
L _____
D _____

Tuesday

B _____
L _____
D _____

Wednesday

B _____
L _____
D _____

Thursday

B _____
L _____
D _____

Friday

B _____
L _____
D _____

Saturday

B _____
L _____
D _____

Sunday

B _____
L _____
D _____

Date _____

Grocery List

Fruits & Veggies	Dairy
Meat	Frozen
Ingredients	Snacks

Snacks

_____
_____
_____
_____
_____
_____

My Goals!

Week:

This weeks Goals

To Do List

Notes

<u>Daily Food Log</u>

Today's Date: _ _ _ _ _ _ _ _ _ _ _ _ _ _ _ _ _

Breakfast

New Foods(s)I tried today....

Lunch

Textures

Smell

Dinner

Color

Hot or Cold

Daily Food Log

Today's Date: _____

Breakfast

New Foods(s)I tried today....

Lunch

Textures

Smell

Dinner

Color

Hot or Cold

Daily Food Log

Today's Date: _ _ _ _ _ _ _ _ _ _ _ _ _ _ _ _ _ _ _

Breakfast

New Foods(s)I tried today....

Lunch

Textures

Smell

Dinner

Color

Hot or Cold

<u>Daily Food Log</u>

Today's Date: _ _ _ _ _ _ _ _ _ _ _ _ _ _ _ _ _ _ _

Breakfast

New Foods(s)I tried today....

Lunch

Textures

Smell

Dinner

Color

Hot or Cold

Daily Food Log

Today's Date: _

Breakfast

New Foods(s)I tried today....

Lunch

Textures

Smell

Dinner

Color

Hot or Cold

Daily Food Log

Today's Date: _____

Breakfast

Lunch

Dinner

New Foods(s)I tried today....

Textures

Smell

Color

Hot or Cold

<u>Daily Food Log</u>

Today's Date: _ _ _ _ _ _ _ _ _ _ _ _ _ _ _ _ _ _ _

Breakfast

New Foods(s)I tried today....

Lunch

Textures

Smell

Dinner

Color

Hot or Cold

My Weekly Emotions Log

Date:	

Choose two words from the list to describe how you felt this week. Feel free to use other words.

angry
annoyed
anxious
ashamed
awkward
brave
calm
cheerful
chill
confused
discouraged
disgusted
distracted
embarrassed
excited
friendly
guilty
happy
hopeful
jealous
lonely
loved
nervous
offended
scared
thoughtful
tired
uncomfortable
unsure
worried

What can cheer you up or help you stay happy and focused?

Anxiety Log

Date _____   Source of Anxiety _____

Time _____   Physical Sensations _____

Place _____

Negative Beliefs

About Yourself	About Situation

What facts do you know are true?

About Yourself	About Situation

Color where you feel
sensations of anxiety

Is there a more balanced way to think about this situation

What has helped before?   ## What is helping now?

Coping Mechanisms

Breathe
Remind yourself that anxiety is just a feeling
Describe your surroundings in detail
Go outdoors
Sip a warm or iced drink slowly
Ground yourself

Monday

B
L
D

Tuesday

B
L
D

Wednesday

B
L
D

Thursday

B
L
D

Friday

B
L
D

Saturday

B
L
D

Sunday

B
L
D

Date _____

Grocery List

Fruits & Veggies	Dairy
Meat	Frozen
Ingredients	Snacks

Snacks

My Goals!

Week:

This weeks Goals

To Do List

Notes

<u>Daily Food Log</u>

Today's Date: _ _ _ _ _ _ _ _ _ _ _ _ _ _ _ _ _ _ _

Breakfast

New Foods(s)I tried today....

Lunch

Textures

Smell

Dinner

Color

Hot or Cold

<u>Daily Food Log</u>

Today's Date: _

Breakfast

New Foods(s)I tried today....

Lunch

Textures

Dinner

Smell

Color

Hot or Cold

Daily Food Log

Today's Date: _ _ _ _ _ _ _ _ _ _ _ _ _ _ _ _ _ _ _

Breakfast

New Foods(s)I tried today....

Lunch

Textures

Smell

Dinner

Color

Hot or Cold

Daily Food Log

Today's Date: _ _ _ _ _ _ _ _ _ _ _ _ _ _ _ _ _ _ _

Breakfast

New Foods(s)I tried today....

Lunch

Textures

Smell

Dinner

Color

Hot or Cold

<u>Daily Food Log</u>

Today's Date: _

Breakfast

New Foods(s)I tried today....

Lunch

Textures

Smell

Dinner

Color

Hot or Cold

<u>Daily Food Log</u>

Today's Date: _ _ _ _ _ _ _ _ _ _ _ _ _ _ _ _ _ _ _

Breakfast

New Foods(s)I tried today....

Lunch

Textures

Smell

Dinner

Color

Hot or Cold

Daily Food Log

Today's Date: _ _ _ _ _ _ _ _ _ _ _ _ _ _ _ _ _ _ _

Breakfast

New Foods(s)I tried today....

Lunch

Textures

Smell

Dinner

Color

Hot or Cold

My Weekly Emotions Log

Date:	

Choose two words from the list to describe how you felt this week. Feel free to use other words.

What can cheer you up or help you stay happy and focused?

angry
annoyed
anxious
ashamed
awkward
brave
calm
cheerful
chill
confused
discouraged
disgusted
distracted
embarrassed
excited
friendly
guilty
happy
hopeful
jealous
lonely
loved
nervous
offended
scared
thoughtful
tired
uncomfortable
unsure
worried

Anxiety Log

Date _____   Source of Anxiety _____

Time _____   Physical Sensations _____

Place _____

Negative Beliefs

About Yourself	About Situation

What facts do you know are true?

About Yourself	About Situation

Color where you feel
sensations of anxiety

Is there a more balanced way to think about this situation

What has helped before?   What is helping now?

Coping Mechanisms

Breathe
Remind yourself that anxiety is just a feeling
Describe your surroundings in detail
Go outdoors
Sip a warm or iced drink slowly
Ground yourself

Monday

B _____
L _____
D _____

Tuesday

B _____
L _____
D _____

Wednesday

B _____
L _____
D _____

Thursday

B _____
L _____
D _____

Friday

B _____
L _____
D _____

Saturday

B _____
L _____
D _____

Sunday

B _____
L _____
D _____

Date _____

Grocery List

Fruits & Veggies	Dairy
Meat	Frozen
Ingredients	Snacks

Snacks

_____
_____
_____
_____
_____

My Goals!

Week:

This weeks Goals

To Do List

Notes

Daily Food Log

Today's Date: _____

Breakfast

New Foods(s)I tried today....

Lunch

Textures

Smell

Dinner

Color

Hot or Cold

Daily Food Log

Today's Date: _____

Breakfast

New Foods(s) I tried today....

Lunch

Textures

Smell

Dinner

Color

Hot or Cold

<u>Daily Food Log</u>

Today's Date: _ _ _ _ _ _ _ _ _ _ _ _ _ _ _ _ _ _ _

Breakfast

New Foods(s)I tried today....

Lunch

Textures

Smell

Dinner

Color

Hot or Cold

<u>Daily Food Log</u>

Today's Date: _ _ _ _ _ _ _ _ _ _ _ _ _ _ _ _ _ _ _

Breakfast

Lunch

Dinner

New Foods(s)I tried today....

Textures

Smell

Color

Hot or Cold

<u>Daily Food Log</u>

Today's Date: _ _ _ _ _ _ _ _ _ _ _ _ _ _ _ _ _ _

Breakfast

New Foods(s)I tried today....

Lunch

Textures

Smell

Dinner

Color

Hot or Cold

Daily Food Log

Today's Date: _ _ _ _ _ _ _ _ _ _ _ _ _ _ _ _ _ _

Breakfast

New Foods(s)I tried today....

Lunch

Textures

Smell

Dinner

Color

Hot or Cold

Daily Food Log

Today's Date: _

Breakfast

New Foods(s)I tried today....

Lunch

Textures

Smell

Dinner

Color

Hot or Cold

<u>My Weekly Emotions Log</u>

Date:	

Choose two words from the list to describe
how you felt this week. Feel free to use other
words.

What can cheer you up or help you stay
happy and focused?

angry
annoyed
anxious
ashamed
awkward
brave
calm
cheerful
chill
confused
discouraged
disgusted
distracted
embarrassed
excited
friendly
guilty
happy
hopeful
jealous
lonely
loved
nervous
offended
scared
thoughtful
tired
uncomfortable
unsure
worried

Anxiety Log

Date _____   Source of Anxiety _____

Time _____   Physical Sensations _____

Place _____

Negative Beliefs

About Yourself	About Situation

What facts do you know are true?

About Yourself	About Situation

Color where you feel sensations of anxiety

Is there a more balanced way to think about this situation

What has helped before?

What is helping now?

Coping Mechanisms

Breathe
Remind yourself that anxiety is just a feeling
Describe your surroundings in detail
Go outdoors
Sip a warm or iced drink slowly
Ground yourself

Monday

B _____
L _____
D _____

Tuesday

B _____
L _____
D _____

Wednesday

B _____
L _____
D _____

Thursday

B _____
L _____
D _____

Friday

B _____
L _____
D _____

Saturday

B _____
L _____
D _____

Sunday

B _____
L _____
D _____

Date _____

Grocery List

Fruits & Veggies	Dairy
Meat	Frozen
Ingredients	Snacks

Snacks

_____
_____
_____
_____

My Goals!

Week:

This weeks Goals

To Do List

Notes

<u>Daily Food Log</u>

Today's Date: _ _ _ _ _ _ _ _ _ _ _ _ _ _ _ _ _ _ _

Breakfast

New Foods(s)I tried today....

Lunch

Textures

Smell

Dinner

Color

Hot or Cold

Daily Food Log

Today's Date: _ _ _ _ _ _ _ _ _ _ _ _ _ _ _ _ _ _ _

Breakfast

New Foods(s)I tried today....

Lunch

Textures

Smell

Dinner

Color

Hot or Cold

<u>Daily Food Log</u>

Today's Date: _ _ _ _ _ _ _ _ _ _ _ _ _ _ _ _ _ _ _

Breakfast

New Foods(s)I tried today....

Lunch

Textures

Smell

Dinner

Color

Hot or Cold

<u>Daily Food Log</u>

Today's Date: _ _ _ _ _ _ _ _ _ _ _ _ _ _ _ _ _ _

Breakfast

New Foods(s)I tried today....

Lunch

Textures

Smell

Dinner

Color

Hot or Cold

☺ 😐 ☹ ><

Daily Food Log

Today's Date: _ _ _ _ _ _ _ _ _ _ _ _ _ _ _ _ _ _ _

Breakfast

New Foods(s)I tried today....

Lunch

Textures

Smell

Dinner

Color

Hot or Cold

<u>Daily Food Log</u>

Today's Date: _ _ _ _ _ _ _ _ _ _ _ _ _ _ _ _ _ _

Breakfast

New Foods(s)I tried today....

Lunch

Textures

Smell

Dinner

Color

Hot or Cold

Daily Food Log

Today's Date: _ _ _ _ _ _ _ _ _ _ _ _ _ _ _ _ _ _

Breakfast

New Foods(s)I tried today....

Lunch

Textures

Smell

Dinner

Color

Hot or Cold

<u>My Weekly Emotions Log</u>

Date:	

Choose two words from the list to describe how you felt this week. Feel free to use other words.

What can cheer you up or help you stay happy and focused?

angry
annoyed
anxious
ashamed
awkward
brave
calm
cheerful
chill
confused
discouraged
disgusted
distracted
embarrassed
excited
friendly
guilty
happy
hopeful
jealous
lonely
loved
nervous
offended
scared
thoughtful
tired
uncomfortable
unsure
worried

<u>Anxiety Log</u>

Date _____   Source of Anxiety _____

Time _____   Physical Sensations _____

Place _____

Negative Beliefs

About Yourself	About Situation

What facts do you know are true?

About Yourself	About Situation

Color where you feel
sensations of anxiety

Is there a more balanced way to think about this situation

What has helped before?

What is helping now?

Coping Mechanisms

Breathe
Remind yourself that anxiety is just a feeling
Describe your surroundings in detail
Go outdoors
Sip a warm or iced drink slowly
Ground yourself

Monday

B _____
L _____
D _____

Tuesday

B _____
L _____
D _____

Wednesday

B _____
L _____
D _____

Thursday

B _____
L _____
D _____

Friday

B _____
L _____
D _____

Saturday

B _____
L _____
D _____

Sunday

B _____
L _____
D _____

Date _____

Grocery List

Fruits & Veggies	Dairy
Meat	Frozen
Ingredients	Snacks

Snacks

_____
_____
_____
_____
_____

My Goals!

Week:

This weeks Goals

To Do List

Notes

<u>Daily Food Log</u>

Today's Date: _ _ _ _ _ _ _ _ _ _ _ _ _ _ _ _ _ _ _

Breakfast

Lunch

Dinner

New Foods(s)I tried today....

Textures

Smell

Color

Hot or Cold

Daily Food Log

Today's Date: _ _ _ _ _ _ _ _ _ _ _ _ _ _ _ _

Breakfast

New Foods(s)I tried today....

Lunch

Textures

Smell

Dinner

Color

Hot or Cold

<u>Daily Food Log</u>

Today's Date: _ _ _ _ _ _ _ _ _ _ _ _ _ _ _ _ _ _

Breakfast

New Foods(s)I tried today....

Lunch

Textures

Smell

Dinner

Color

Hot or Cold

Daily Food Log

Today's Date: _

Breakfast

New Foods(s)I tried today....

Lunch

Textures

Smell

Dinner

Color

Hot or Cold

<u>Daily Food Log</u>

Today's Date: _ _ _ _ _ _ _ _ _ _ _ _ _ _ _ _ _ _ _

Breakfast

Lunch

Dinner

New Foods(s)I tried today....

Textures

Smell

Color

Hot or Cold

<u>Daily Food Log</u>

Today's Date: _ _ _ _ _ _ _ _ _ _ _ _ _ _ _ _ _ _ _

Breakfast

Lunch

Dinner

New Foods(s)I tried today....

Textures

Smell

Color

Hot or Cold

Daily Food Log

Today's Date: _ _ _ _ _ _ _ _ _ _ _ _ _ _ _ _ _ _ _

Breakfast

New Foods(s)I tried today....

Lunch

Textures

Smell

Dinner

Color

Hot or Cold

My Weekly Emotions Log

Date:	

Choose two words from the list to describe how you felt this week. Feel free to use other words.

angry
annoyed
anxious
ashamed
awkward
brave
calm
cheerful
chill
confused
discouraged
disgusted
distracted
embarrassed
excited
friendly
guilty
happy
hopeful
jealous
lonely
loved
nervous
offended
scared
thoughtful
tired
uncomfortable
unsure
worried

What can cheer you up or help you stay happy and focused?

Anxiety Log

Date _____

Source of Anxiety _____

Time _____

Physical Sensations _____

Place _____

Negative Beliefs

About Yourself	About Situation

What facts do you know are true?

About Yourself	About Situation

Color where you feel
sensations of anxiety

Is there a more balanced way to think about this situation

What has helped before?

What is helping now?

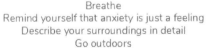

Coping Mechanisms

Breathe
Remind yourself that anxiety is just a feeling
Describe your surroundings in detail
Go outdoors
Sip a warm or iced drink slowly
Ground yourself

Monday

B _____
L _____
D _____

Tuesday

B _____
L _____
D _____

Wednesday

B _____
L _____
D _____

Thursday

B _____
L _____
D _____

Friday

B _____
L _____
D _____

Saturday

B _____
L _____
D _____

Sunday

B _____
L _____
D _____

Date _____

Grocery List

Fruits & Veggies	Dairy
Meat	Frozen
Ingredients	Snacks

Snacks

_____
_____
_____
_____

My Goals!

Week:

This weeks Goals

To Do List

Notes

Daily Food Log

Today's Date: _____

Breakfast

New Foods(s)I tried today....

Lunch

Textures

Dinner

Smell

Color

Hot or Cold

<u>Daily Food Log</u>

Today's Date: _ _ _ _ _ _ _ _ _ _ _ _ _ _ _ _ _ _ _

Breakfast

Lunch

Dinner

New Foods(s)I tried today....

Textures

Smell

Color

Hot or Cold

<u>Daily Food Log</u>

Today's Date: _ _ _ _ _ _ _ _ _ _ _ _ _ _ _ _ _ _ _

Breakfast

New Foods(s)I tried today....

Lunch

Textures

Smell

Dinner

Color

Hot or Cold

<u>Daily Food Log</u>

Today's Date: _ _ _ _ _ _ _ _ _ _ _ _ _ _ _ _ _ _ _

Breakfast

New Foods(s)I tried today....

Lunch

Textures

Smell

Dinner

Color

Hot or Cold

<u>Daily Food Log</u>

Today's Date: _ _ _ _ _ _ _ _ _ _ _ _ _ _ _ _ _ _ _

Breakfast

New Foods(s)I tried today....

Lunch

Textures

Smell

Dinner

Color

Hot or Cold

Daily Food Log

Today's Date: _ _ _ _ _ _ _ _ _ _ _ _ _ _ _ _ _ _ _

Breakfast

New Foods(s)I tried today....

Lunch

Textures

Smell

Dinner

Color

Hot or Cold

<u>Daily Food Log</u>

Today's Date: _____

Breakfast

New Foods(s)I tried today....

Lunch

Textures

Dinner

Smell

Color

Hot or Cold

My Weekly Emotions Log

Date:	

Choose two words from the list to describe how you felt this week. Feel free to use other words.

angry
annoyed
anxious
ashamed
awkward
brave
calm
cheerful
chill
confused
discouraged
disgusted
distracted
embarrassed

What can cheer you up or help you stay happy and focused?

excited
friendly
guilty
happy
hopeful
jealous
lonely
loved
nervous
offended
scared
thoughtful
tired
uncomfortable
unsure
worried

Anxiety Log

Date _____   Source of Anxiety _____

Time _____   Physical Sensations _____

Place _____

Negative Beliefs

About Yourself	About Situation

What facts do you know are true?

About Yourself	About Situation

Color where you feel
sensations of anxiety

Is there a more balanced way to think about this situation

What has helped before?   What is helping now?

Coping Mechanisms

Breathe
Remind yourself that anxiety is just a feeling
Describe your surroundings in detail
Go outdoors
Sip a warm or iced drink slowly
Ground yourself

Monday

B _____
L _____
D _____

Tuesday

B _____
L _____
D _____

Wednesday

B _____
L _____
D _____

Thursday

B _____
L _____
D _____

Friday

B _____
L _____
D _____

Saturday

B _____
L _____
D _____

Sunday

B _____
L _____
D _____

Date _____

Grocery List

Fruits & Veggies	Dairy
Meat	Frozen
Ingredients	Snacks

Snacks

_____
_____
_____
_____
_____

My Goals!

Week:

This weeks Goals

To Do List

Notes

Daily Food Log

Today's Date: _ _ _ _ _ _ _ _ _ _ _ _ _ _ _ _ _ _ _

Breakfast

New Foods(s)I tried today....

Lunch

Textures

Smell

Dinner

Color

Hot or Cold

<u>Daily Food Log</u>

Today's Date: _ _ _ _ _ _ _ _ _ _ _ _ _ _ _ _ _ _ _

Breakfast

New Foods(s)I tried today....

Lunch

Textures

Smell

Dinner

Color

Hot or Cold

Daily Food Log

Today's Date: _ _ _ _ _ _ _ _ _ _ _ _ _ _ _ _ _ _ _

Breakfast

New Foods(s)I tried today....

Lunch

Textures

Smell

Dinner

Color

Hot or Cold

Daily Food Log

Today's Date: _____

Breakfast

Lunch

Dinner

New Foods(s)I tried today....

Textures

Smell

Color

Hot or Cold

<u>Daily Food Log</u>

Today's Date: _ _ _ _ _ _ _ _ _ _ _ _ _ _ _ _ _ _ _

Breakfast

New Foods(s)I tried today....

Lunch

Textures

Smell

Dinner

Color

Hot or Cold

<u>Daily</u> Food Log

Today's Date: _ _ _ _ _ _ _ _ _ _ _ _ _ _ _ _ _ _ _

Breakfast

New Foods(s)I tried today....

Lunch

Textures

Smell

Dinner

Color

Hot or Cold

Daily Food Log

Today's Date: _ _ _ _ _ _ _ _ _ _ _ _ _ _ _ _ _ _ _

Breakfast

New Foods(s)I tried today....

Lunch

Textures

Smell

Dinner

Color

Hot or Cold

My Weekly Emotions Log

Date:

Choose two words from the list to describe how you felt this week. Feel free to use other words.

What can cheer you up or help you stay happy and focused?

angry
annoyed
anxious
ashamed
awkward
brave
calm
cheerful
chill
confused
discouraged
disgusted
distracted
embarrassed
excited
friendly
guilty
happy
hopeful
jealous
lonely
loved
nervous
offended
scared
thoughtful
tired
uncomfortable
unsure
worried

Anxiety Log

Date _____   Source of Anxiety _____

Time _____   Physical Sensations _____

Place _____

Negative Beliefs

About Yourself	About Situation

What facts do you know are true?

About Yourself	About Situation

Color where you feel
sensations of anxiety

Is there a more balanced way to think about this situation

What has helped before?   What is helping now?

Coping Mechanisms

Breathe
Remind yourself that anxiety is just a feeling
Describe your surroundings in detail
Go outdoors
Sip a warm or iced drink slowly
Ground yourself

Monday

B _____
L _____
D _____

Tuesday

B _____
L _____
D _____

Wednesday

B _____
L _____
D _____

Thursday

B _____
L _____
D _____

Friday

B _____
L _____
D _____

Saturday

B _____
L _____
D _____

Sunday

B _____
L _____
D _____

Date _____

Grocery List

Fruits & Veggies	Dairy
Meat	Frozen
Ingredients	Snacks

Snacks

_____
_____
_____
_____
_____

My Goals!

Week:

This weeks Goals

To Do List

Notes

Daily Food Log

Today's Date: _____

Breakfast

New Foods(s)I tried today....

Lunch

Textures

Smell

Dinner

Color

Hot or Cold

<u>Daily Food Log</u>

Today's Date: _ _ _ _ _ _ _ _ _ _ _ _ _ _ _ _ _ _ _

Breakfast

New Foods(s)I tried today....

Lunch

Textures

Smell

Dinner

Color

Hot or Cold

Daily Food Log

Today's Date: _ _ _ _ _ _ _ _ _ _ _ _ _ _ _ _ _

Breakfast

New Foods(s)I tried today....

Lunch

Textures

Smell

Dinner

Color

Hot or Cold

Daily Food Log

Today's Date: _

Breakfast

New Foods(s)I tried today....

Lunch

Textures

Smell

Dinner

Color

Hot or Cold

<u>Daily Food Log</u>

Today's Date: _ _ _ _ _ _ _ _ _ _ _ _ _ _ _ _ _ _

Breakfast

New Foods(s)I tried today....

Lunch

Textures

Smell

Dinner

Color

Hot or Cold

<u>Daily Food Log</u>

Today's Date: _ _ _ _ _ _ _ _ _ _ _ _ _ _ _

Breakfast

New Foods(s)I tried today....

Lunch

Textures

Smell

Dinner

Color

Hot or Cold

Daily Food Log

Today's Date: _

Breakfast

New Foods(s)I tried today....

Lunch

Textures

Smell

Dinner

Color

Hot or Cold

My Weekly Emotions Log

Date:	

Choose two words from the list to describe how you felt this week. Feel free to use other words.

What can cheer you up or help you stay happy and focused?

angry
annoyed
anxious
ashamed
awkward
brave
calm
cheerful
chill
confused
discouraged
disgusted
distracted
embarrassed
excited
friendly
guilty
happy
hopeful
jealous
lonely
loved
nervous
offended
scared
thoughtful
tired
uncomfortable
unsure
worried

Anxiety Log

Date _____   Source of Anxiety _____

Time _____   Physical Sensations _____

Place _____

Negative Beliefs

About Yourself	About Situation

What facts do you know are true?

About Yourself	About Situation

Color where you feel
sensations of anxiety

Is there a more balanced way to think about this situation

What has helped before?

What is helping now?

Coping Mechanisms

Breathe
Remind yourself that anxiety is just a feeling
Describe your surroundings in detail
Go outdoors
Sip a warm or iced drink slowly
Ground yourself

Monday

B _____

L _____

D _____

Tuesday

B _____

L _____

D _____

Wednesday

B _____

L _____

D _____

Thursday

B _____

L _____

D _____

Friday

B _____

L _____

D _____

Saturday

B _____

L _____

D _____

Sunday

B _____

L _____

D _____

Date _____

Grocery List

Fruits & Veggies	Dairy
Meat	Frozen
Ingredients	Snacks

Snacks

_____

_____

_____

_____

My Goals!

Week:

This weeks Goals

To Do List

Notes

Daily Food Log

Today's Date: _ _ _ _ _ _ _ _ _ _ _ _ _ _ _ _ _ _

Breakfast

New Foods(s)I tried today....

Lunch

Textures

Smell

Dinner

Color

Hot or Cold

<u>Daily Food Log</u>

Today's Date:

- - - - - - - - - - - - - - - - - - -

Breakfast

New Foods(s)I tried today....

Lunch

Textures

Smell

Dinner

Color

Hot or Cold

<u>Daily Food Log</u>

Today's Date: _ _ _ _ _ _ _ _ _ _ _ _ _ _ _ _ _

Breakfast

New Foods(s)I tried today....

Lunch

Textures

Smell

Dinner

Color

Hot or Cold

Daily Food Log

Today's Date: _

Breakfast

New Foods(s)I tried today....

Lunch

Textures

Smell

Dinner

Color

Hot or Cold

<u>Daily Food Log</u>

Today's Date: _ _ _ _ _ _ _ _ _ _ _ _ _ _ _ _ _ _

Breakfast

Lunch

Dinner

New Foods(s)I tried today....

Textures

Smell

Color

Hot or Cold

Daily Food Log

Today's Date: _____

Breakfast

New Foods(s)I tried today....

Lunch

Textures

Smell

Dinner

Color

Hot or Cold

<u>Daily Food Log</u>

Today's Date: _ _ _ _ _ _ _ _ _ _ _ _ _ _ _ _ _ _

Breakfast

New Foods(s)I tried today....

Lunch

Textures

Smell

Dinner

Color

Hot or Cold

My Weekly Emotions Log

Date:

Choose two words from the list to describe how you felt this week. Feel free to use other words.

angry
annoyed
anxious
ashamed
awkward
brave
calm
cheerful
chill
confused
discouraged
disgusted
distracted
embarrassed
excited
friendly
guilty
happy
hopeful
jealous
lonely
loved
nervous
offended
scared
thoughtful
tired
uncomfortable
unsure
worried

What can cheer you up or help you stay happy and focused?

Anxiety Log

Date _____   Source of Anxiety _____

Time _____   Physical Sensations _____

Place _____

Negative Beliefs

About Yourself	About Situation

What facts do you know are true?

About Yourself	About Situation

Color where you feel
sensations of anxiety

Is there a more balanced way to think about this situation

What has helped before?   What is helping now?

Coping Mechanisms

Breathe
Remind yourself that anxiety is just a feeling
Describe your surroundings in detail
Go outdoors
Sip a warm or iced drink slowly
Ground yourself

Monday

B
L
D

Tuesday

B
L
D

Wednesday

B
L
D

Thursday

B
L
D

Friday

B
L
D

Saturday

B
L
D

Sunday

B
L
D

Date

Grocery List

Fruits & Veggies	Dairy
Meat	Frozen
Ingredients	Snacks

Snacks

My Goals!

Week:

This weeks Goals

To Do List

Notes

Daily Food Log

Today's Date: _ _ _ _ _ _ _ _ _ _ _ _ _ _ _ _ _ _ _

Breakfast

New Foods(s)I tried today....

Lunch

Textures

Dinner

Smell

Color

Hot or Cold

☺ 😐 ☹ >_<

<u>Daily Food Log</u>

Today's Date: _ _ _ _ _ _ _ _ _ _ _ _ _ _ _ _ _ _ _

Breakfast

New Foods(s)I tried today....

Lunch

Textures

Smell

Dinner

Color

Hot or Cold

Daily Food Log

Today's Date: _____

Breakfast

New Foods(s)I tried today....

Lunch

Textures

Dinner

Smell

Color

Hot or Cold

<u>Daily Food Log</u>

Today's Date: _ _ _ _ _ _ _ _ _ _ _ _ _ _ _ _ _ _

Breakfast

Lunch

Dinner

New Foods(s)I tried today....

Textures

Smell

Color

Hot or Cold

Daily Food Log

Today's Date: _ _ _ _ _ _ _ _ _ _ _ _ _ _ _ _ _ _ _

Breakfast

New Foods(s)I tried today....

Lunch

Textures

Smell

Dinner

Color

Hot or Cold

<u>Daily Food Log</u>

Today's Date: _ _ _ _ _ _ _ _ _ _ _ _ _ _ _ _ _ _

Breakfast

New Foods(s)I tried today....

Lunch

Textures

Smell

Dinner

Color

Hot or Cold

<u>Daily Food Log</u>

Today's Date: _ _ _ _ _ _ _ _ _ _ _ _ _ _ _ _ _ _ _

Breakfast

New Foods(s)I tried today....

Lunch

Textures

Smell

Dinner

Color

Hot or Cold

<u>My Weekly Emotions Log</u>

Date:	

Choose two words from the list to describe how you felt this week. Feel free to use other words.

What can cheer you up or help you stay happy and focused?

angry
annoyed
anxious
ashamed
awkward
brave
calm
cheerful
chill
confused
discouraged
disgusted
distracted
embarrassed
excited
friendly
guilty
happy
hopeful
jealous
lonely
loved
nervous
offended
scared
thoughtful
tired
uncomfortable
unsure
worried

Anxiety Log

Date _____   Source of Anxiety _____

Time _____   Physical Sensations _____

Place _____

Negative Beliefs

About Yourself	About Situation

What facts do you know are true?

About Yourself	About Situation

Color where you feel
sensations of anxiety

Is there a more balanced way to think about this situation

What has helped before?

What is helping now?

―――――――― Coping Mechanisms ――――――――

Breathe
Remind yourself that anxiety is just a feeling
Describe your surroundings in detail
Go outdoors
Sip a warm or iced drink slowly
Ground yourself

Monday

B \
L \
D

Tuesday

B \
L \
D

Wednesday

B \
L \
D

Thursday

B \
L \
D

Friday

B \
L \
D

Saturday

B \
L \
D

Sunday

B \
L \
D

Date

Grocery List

Fruits & Veggies	Dairy
Meat	Frozen
Ingredients	Snacks

Snacks

My Goals!

Week:

This weeks Goals

To Do List

Notes

<u>Daily Food Log</u>

Today's Date: _ _ _ _ _ _ _ _ _ _ _ _ _ _ _ _ _ _ _

Breakfast

Lunch

Dinner

New Foods(s)I tried today....

Textures

Smell

Color

Hot or Cold

<u>Daily Food Log</u>

Today's Date: _ _ _ _ _ _ _ _ _ _ _ _ _ _ _

Breakfast

New Foods(s)I tried today....

Lunch

Textures

Smell

Dinner

Color

Hot or Cold

<u>Daily Food Log</u>

Today's Date: _ _ _ _ _ _ _ _ _ _ _ _ _ _ _ _ _ _ _

Breakfast

New Foods(s)I tried today....

Lunch

Textures

Smell

Dinner

Color

Hot or Cold

Daily Food Log

Today's Date: _____

Breakfast

Lunch

Dinner

New Foods(s) I tried today....

Textures

Smell

Color

Hot or Cold

<u>Daily Food Log</u>

Today's Date: _____

Breakfast

New Foods(s)I tried today....

Lunch

Textures

Smell

Dinner

Color

Hot or Cold

<u>Daily Food Log</u>

Today's Date: _ _ _ _ _ _ _ _ _ _ _ _ _ _ _ _ _ _ _

Breakfast

New Foods(s) I tried today....

Lunch

Textures

Smell

Dinner

Color

Hot or Cold

<u>Daily Food Log</u>

Today's Date: _ _ _ _ _ _ _ _ _ _ _ _ _ _ _ _ _ _ _

Breakfast

New Foods(s)I tried today....

Lunch

Textures

Smell

Dinner

Color

Hot or Cold

My Weekly Emotions Log

Date:

Choose two words from the list to describe how you felt this week. Feel free to use other words.

What can cheer you up or help you stay happy and focused?

angry
annoyed
anxious
ashamed
awkward
brave
calm
cheerful
chill
confused
discouraged
disgusted
distracted
embarrassed
excited
friendly
guilty
happy
hopeful
jealous
lonely
loved
nervous
offended
scared
thoughtful
tired
uncomfortable
unsure
worried

<u>Anxiety Log</u>

Date _____   Source of Anxiety _____

Time _____   Physical Sensations _____

Place _____

Negative Beliefs

About Yourself	About Situation

What facts do you know are true?

About Yourself	About Situation

Color where you feel
sensations of anxiety

Is there a more balanced way to think about this situation

What has helped before?   What is helping now?

── Coping Mechanisms ──

Breathe
Remind yourself that anxiety is just a feeling
Describe your surroundings in detail
Go outdoors
Sip a warm or iced drink slowly
Ground yourself

Monday

B _____

L _____

D _____

Tuesday

B _____

L _____

D _____

Wednesday

B _____

L _____

D _____

Thursday

B _____

L _____

D _____

Friday

B _____

L _____

D _____

Saturday

B _____

L _____

D _____

Sunday

B _____

L _____

D _____

Date _____

Grocery List

Fruits & Veggies	Dairy
Meat	Frozen
Ingredients	Snacks

Snacks

_____

_____

_____

_____

_____

My Goals!

Week:

This weeks Goals

To Do List

Notes

Daily Food Log

Today's Date: _ _ _ _ _ _ _ _ _ _ _ _ _ _ _ _ _ _

Breakfast

New Foods(s)I tried today....

Lunch

Textures

Smell

Dinner

Color

Hot or Cold

Daily Food Log

Today's Date: _ _ _ _ _ _ _ _ _ _ _ _ _ _ _ _ _

Breakfast

Lunch

Dinner

New Foods(s) I tried today....

Textures

Smell

Color

Hot or Cold

<u>Daily Food Log</u>

Today's Date: _ _ _ _ _ _ _ _ _ _ _ _ _ _ _ _ _ _ _

Breakfast

New Foods(s)I tried today....

Lunch

Textures

Smell

Dinner.

Color

Hot or Cold

<u>Daily Food Log</u>

Today's Date: _ _ _ _ _ _ _ _ _ _ _ _ _ _ _ _ _ _ _

Breakfast

New Foods(s)I tried today....

Lunch

Textures

Smell

Dinner

Color

Hot or Cold

<u>Daily Food Log</u>

Today's Date: _ _ _ _ _ _ _ _ _ _ _ _ _ _ _ _ _ _ _

Breakfast

New Foods(s)I tried today....

Lunch

Textures

Smell

Dinner

Color

Hot or Cold

<u>Daily Food Log</u>

Today's Date: _ _ _ _ _ _ _ _ _ _ _ _ _ _ _ _ _ _

Breakfast

New Foods(s)I tried today....

Lunch

Textures

Smell

Dinner

Color

Hot or Cold

Daily Food Log

Today's Date: _____

Breakfast

New Foods(s)I tried today....

Lunch

Textures

Smell

Dinner

Color

Hot or Cold

My Weekly Emotions Log

Date:	

Choose two words from the list to describe how you felt this week. Feel free to use other words.

What can cheer you up or help you stay happy and focused?

angry
annoyed
anxious
ashamed
awkward
brave
calm
cheerful
chill
confused
discouraged
disgusted
distracted
embarrassed
excited
friendly
guilty
happy
hopeful
jealous
lonely
loved
nervous
offended
scared
thoughtful
tired
uncomfortable
unsure
worried

Anxiety Log

Date _____   Source of Anxiety _____

Time _____   Physical Sensations _____

Place _____

Negative Beliefs

About Yourself	About Situation

What facts do you know are true?

About Yourself	About Situation

Color where you feel
sensations of anxiety

Is there a more balanced way to think about this situation

What has helped before?

What is helping now?

—————— Coping Mechanisms ——————
Breathe
Remind yourself that anxiety is just a feeling
Describe your surroundings in detail
Go outdoors
Sip a warm or iced drink slowly
Ground yourself

Monday

B _____

L _____

D _____

Tuesday

B _____

L _____

D _____

Wednesday

B _____

L _____

D _____

Thursday

B _____

L _____

D _____

Friday

B _____

L _____

D _____

Saturday

B _____

L _____

D _____

Sunday

B _____

L _____

D _____

Date _____

Grocery List

Fruits & Veggies	Dairy
Meat	Frozen
Ingredients	Snacks

Snacks

_____

_____

_____

_____

_____

My Goals!

Week:

This weeks Goals

To Do List

Notes

Daily Food Log

Today's Date: _ _ _ _ _ _ _ _ _ _ _ _ _ _ _ _ _ _

Breakfast

New Foods(s)I tried today....

Lunch

Textures

Smell

Dinner

Color

Hot or Cold

Daily Food Log

Today's Date: _ _ _ _ _ _ _ _ _ _ _ _ _ _ _ _ _ _ _

Breakfast

New Foods(s)I tried today....

Lunch

Textures

Smell

Dinner

Color

Hot or Cold

<u>Daily Food Log</u>

Today's Date: _ _ _ _ _ _ _ _ _ _ _ _ _ _ _ _ _

Breakfast

New Foods(s)I tried today....

Lunch

Textures

Smell

Dinner

Color

Hot or Cold

<u>Daily Food Log</u>

Today's Date: _ _ _ _ _ _ _ _ _ _ _ _ _ _ _ _ _ _ _

Breakfast

New Foods(s)I tried today....

Lunch

Textures

Smell

Dinner

Color

Hot or Cold

Daily Food Log

Today's Date: _ _ _ _ _ _ _ _ _ _ _ _ _ _ _ _ _

Breakfast

New Foods(s)I tried today....

Lunch

Textures

Smell

Dinner

Color

Hot or Cold

<u>Daily Food Log</u>

Today's Date: _____

Breakfast

New Foods(s)I tried today....

Lunch

Textures

Smell

Dinner

Color

Hot or Cold

<u>Daily Food Log</u>

Today's Date: _ _ _ _ _ _ _ _ _ _ _ _ _ _ _ _ _ _

Breakfast

New Foods(s)I tried today....

Lunch

Textures

Smell

Dinner

Color

Hot or Cold

My Weekly Emotions Log

Date:	

Choose two words from the list to describe how you felt this week. Feel free to use other words.

What can cheer you up or help you stay happy and focused?

angry
annoyed
anxious
ashamed
awkward
brave
calm
cheerful
chill
confused
discouraged
disgusted
distracted
embarrassed
excited
friendly
guilty
happy
hopeful
jealous
lonely
loved
nervous
offended
scared
thoughtful
tired
uncomfortable
unsure
worried

<u>Anxiety Log</u>

Date _____   Source of Anxiety _____

Time _____   Physical Sensations _____

Place _____

Negative Beliefs

About Yourself	About Situation

What facts do you know are true?

About Yourself	About Situation

Color where you feel
sensations of anxiety

Is there a more balanced way to think about this situation

What has helped before?

What is helping now?

Coping Mechanisms

Breathe
Remind yourself that anxiety is just a feeling
Describe your surroundings in detail
Go outdoors
Sip a warm or iced drink slowly
Ground yourself

Monday

B _____
L _____
D _____

Tuesday

B _____
L _____
D _____

Wednesday

B _____
L _____
D _____

Thursday

B _____
L _____
D _____

Friday

B _____
L _____
D _____

Saturday

B _____
L _____
D _____

Sunday

B _____
L _____
D _____

Date _____

Grocery List

Fruits & Veggies	Dairy
Meat	Frozen
Ingredients	Snacks

Snacks

_____
_____
_____
_____

My Goals!

Week:

This weeks Goals

To Do List

Notes

<u>Daily Food Log</u>

Today's Date: _ _ _ _ _ _ _ _ _ _ _ _ _ _ _ _ _ _ _

Breakfast

New Foods(s)I tried today....

Lunch

Textures

Smell

Dinner

Color

Hot or Cold

Daily Food Log

Today's Date: _ _ _ _ _ _ _ _ _ _ _ _ _ _ _ _ _ _ _

Breakfast

New Foods(s)I tried today....

Lunch

Textures

Smell

Dinner

Color

Hot or Cold

<u>Daily Food Log</u>

Today's Date: _

Breakfast

New Foods(s)I tried today....

Lunch

Textures

Smell

Dinner

Color

Hot or Cold

Daily Food Log

Today's Date: _ _ _ _ _ _ _ _ _ _ _ _ _ _ _ _ _ _ _

Breakfast

New Foods(s)I tried today....

Lunch

Textures

Smell

Dinner

Color

Hot or Cold

Daily Food Log

Today's Date: _ _ _ _ _ _ _ _ _ _ _ _ _ _ _ _ _ _

Breakfast

New Foods(s)I tried today....

Lunch

Textures

Smell

Dinner

Color

Hot or Cold

<u>Daily Food Log</u>

Today's Date: _____

Breakfast

New Foods(s)I tried today....

Lunch

Textures

Smell

Dinner

Color

Hot or Cold

😊 😐 🙁 😖

Daily Food Log

Today's Date: - - - - - - - - - - - - - - - - - - -

Breakfast

New Foods(s)I tried today....

Lunch

Textures

Smell

Dinner

Color

Hot or Cold

My Weekly Emotions Log

Date:	

Choose two words from the list to describe how you felt this week. Feel free to use other words.

What can cheer you up or help you stay happy and focused?

angry
annoyed
anxious
ashamed
awkward
brave
calm
cheerful
chill
confused
discouraged
disgusted
distracted
embarrassed
excited
friendly
guilty
happy
hopeful
jealous
lonely
loved
nervous
offended
scared
thoughtful
tired
uncomfortable
unsure
worried

Anxiety Log

Date _____   Source of Anxiety _____

Time _____   Physical Sensations _____

Place _____

Negative Beliefs

About Yourself	About Situation

What facts do you know are true?

About Yourself	About Situation

Color where you feel
sensations of anxiety

Is there a more balanced way to think about this situation

What has helped before?

What is helping now?

Coping Mechanisms

Breathe
Remind yourself that anxiety is just a feeling
Describe your surroundings in detail
Go outdoors
Sip a warm or iced drink slowly
Ground yourself